# The Complete Mediterranean Meal Prep Guide:

Time Saving Recipes for the World's Healthiest Diet

By: Maureen Sarkis

© Copyright 2018 by Maureen Sarkis - All rights reserved.

# Contents:

Introduction:   6

The Mediterranean Diet:   9

What is the Mediterranean Diet?   9

Amazing Benefits of the Mediterranean Diet: 10

What to Eat and What to Avoid:   13

7 Steps for Success in the Mediterranean Diet:   15

Meal Prepping:   18

10 Tips to make you an Expert in Food Prepping:   21

Some considerations regarding food prepping safety:   34

Breakfast/Brunch Recipes:   37

1). Tuscan Vegetable Frittata: 37

2). Mediterranean Cranberry Breakfast Muffins:   39

3). Slow Cooker Breakfast Quinoa with Blueberries:   41

4). Greek Yogurt Parfait   43

5). Breakfast Polenta with Banana   45

6). Shakshukah Breakfast Skillet:   47

8). Greek Omelet   49

9). Honey Walnut Overnight Oats:   51

10). Mango Strawberry Breakfast Smoothie with Yogurt   53

Lunch Recipes: 55

1). Mediterranean Quinoa Spinach Salad in a Jar   55

2). Garbanzo Egg Salad with Honey Dijon Vinaigrette 58

3). Tuna Salad Avocado Boats 60

4). Classic Greek Salad in a Jar 62

5). Pork Loin and Orzo: 64

6). Tuna and White Bean Lettuce Wraps 66

7). Warm Tuscan Artichoke Salad 68

8). Roasted Zucchini with Yogurt and Dill 70

9). Roasted Red Pepper Hummus with Fresh Veggies 72

10). Greek Tacos: 74

11). Turkey Lentil Meatballs with Tzatziki Dipping Sauce 76

12). Chilled Artichoke Zucchini Salad 78

13). White Bean Soup 80

14). Balsamic Beet Salad with Blue Cheese and Walnuts 82

15) Lebanese Tabbouleh 84

Dinner Recipes: 86

1). Stuffed Peppers: 86

2). Slow Cooker Pork Tenderloin with Quinoa Salad 89

3). Spinach Pasta Fazool 92

4). Zesty Lentil Zuppa Toscana 94

5). Pan Seared Eggplant Medallions with Balsamic Reduction 97

6). Oven Roasted Garlic Chicken Thighs 99

7). Roasted Carrot Ginger Bisque 101

8). Garlic Lentil Bowls 103

9). Balsamic Chicken Skewers with Summer Vegetables 105

10). Caprese Stuffed Chicken 107

11). Mediterranean Quinoa Bake         109

12). Slow Cooker Honey Garlic Chicken Thighs         112

13). Spaghetti Squash and Meatballs 113

14). Lemon Salmon with White Beans         116

15). Grilled Chicken with Homemade Tzatziki 118

16). Cauliflower Prawn Casserole         120

17). Halibut Beurre Blanc         123

18). Polenta With Roasted Summer Vegetables         125

19). Spanakopita Egg Bake         127

20). Vegetable Thin Crust Pizza         129

21). One-Pan Honey Lemon Chicken         132

22). Harvest Pumpkin Lentil Soup         135

23). Zoodle Greek Pasta Salad 137

24). Oven Baked Stuffed Zucchini         140

25). Eggplant Pesto Casserole 142

Conclusion:         145

# Introduction:

It would be a mistake to think (when considering the Mediterranean diet)that it is as a traditional "diet." Because quite honestly, it's not a diet. It's a way of eating and a lifestyle. People in the Mediterranean region have been eating this way for centuries and have been enjoying the wonderful health benefits almost unintentionally. That's the joy of this lifestyle — it's almost effortless. You don't have the unnatural side effects, chemical imbalances or hunger that you experience when following other diet regimens because this lifestyle focuses on adding nutrients to your diet instead of taking them away.

If you're reading this book, it's probably a safe assumption that you've already done a fair amount of research on the Mediterranean diet and you may have already implemented it in your own life. The purpose of this book isn't simply to educate you on Mediterranean cooking and eating, but to provide you with the tools that are essential to making this diet work for your life instead of being a burden or a goal you're always falling short of.

In today's society, it is so easy to spend so much of our time feeling like failures. We see everyone's perfect lives on TV, or on social media and we always can't help but compare our own lives and feel that we're always falling short. No matter how far we've come there always seems to be someone that has accomplished more or done it in less time than us. I struggle with this in my own life. When I made some major lifestyle changes and changed my eating habits and managed to lose 40 pounds in 1 summer and continued to be in the best shape of my life, I still felt like a failure. There were always people that had better bodies than me or had lost even more weight etc.

So where am I going with all of this? At the risk of getting philosophical in a recipe book, one rule I've come to live by has helped me immensely. Comparison is the thief of joy. We make ourselves miserable by comparing ourselves to others and we are robbing ourselves of enjoying our own little victories and successes when we try to measure up to others.

That's one of the things I love about the Mediterranean diet. It's not just a list of rules about what you can and cannot eat, it's a mentality. If you adopt the Mediterranean way of eating into your lifestyle, you should also adopt the Mediterranean outlook on life. This is an attitude that says "life's too short to sweat the small stuff." You should be able to enjoy your food, feel good about the food you're eating and of course, share it with the ones you love the most.

It really won't feel like a diet as you're sipping a glass of red wine that compliments the sharpness of feta, balances the sweetness of dates and sweetens the saltiness of fresh olives. One bite of these delicious recipes and you'll feel transported. When you sit down to dinner, it will be easy to picture yourself in an al fresco courtyard along the Mediterranean coast. Or else strolling in a sunlit vineyard in old world Tuscany. But don't take my word for it, read on and see for yourself.

# The Mediterranean Diet:

## *What is the Mediterranean Diet?*

First let's start with what this diet is not:

- It is not a list of rules about what you can and cannot eat
- It's not a death sentence to flavor and enjoyable food
- It's not a restrictive diet that will leave you with only a few types of foods you can eat
- It doesn't require expensive supplements, ingredients or equipment

As stated in the introduction, less of a diet and more of a lifestyle, the Mediterranean way of eating focuses on enriching your diet with fruits and vegetables, grains, beans, and fish foods that have been linked to a whole host of amazing health benefits. The Mediterranean diet is regularly praised by scientists as one of the healthiest diets of all time.

# *Amazing Benefits of the Mediterranean Diet:*

There are many reasons why someone might decide to implement the Mediterranean Diet into their life, and weight loss is only the beginning. While it is true, that you can experience amazing weight loss benefits from following the Mediterranean diet there are many other benefits you may not be aware of.

- **NATURAL WEIGHT LOSS:** Weight loss, but the Natural Way: you are not starving yourself on this diet nor will you find yourself hungry all the time as you would on most other diets. You are not depriving yourself of necessary nutrients the way other diets do sometimes. One of the big differentiators here is the consumption of "healthy fats." This is what leaves you feeling full and satiated without having a negative impact on your health or weight.

- **NUTRIENT RICH FOOD:** An increase in probiotics, quality proteins, vitamins, omega-threes and other healthy nutrients and minerals that can be deficient in other diets.

- **HEART HEALTH**: some people may even be "prescribed" this diet by their doctor for the amazing heart-health benefits.

Some studies have found that this healthy consumption of mono-unsaturated fats and increase in good cholesterol, plus the increase in omega-threes have been found to likely decrease cardiac death rates by up to 45%

- **DIABETES PREVENTION AND CURE:** Roughly 10% of Americans struggle with diabetes. This is an astounding figure especially when comparing to the stats of people living in the Mediterranean countries. The Mediterranean diet has long been seen as a natural cure for certain types of diabetes because it is naturally low in sugar—and almost completely devoid of processed sugar, and high in fresh fruits and vegetables as well as healthy fats.

- **CANCER PREVENTION:** The high concentration of health fatty acids, as well as antioxidants and fiber have led many to see a link between the Mediterranean diet and cancer prevention. Plus, this diet is completely devoid of processed foods which are often filled with chemicals that have been linked to cancerous growth.

- **ANTI-AGING:** Some studies have shown decreased muscle deterioration in the elderly by up to 60%. Also, there have been many studies linking this type of diet with Alzheimer's and dementia prevention making the Mediterranean diet one of the best diets for anti-aging.

Adoption of this diet in regions outside of the Mediterranean started after a post World War II study on world diets conducted by a team of scientists. Actually, the residents of Crete ranked as the number 1 healthiest group in the study. There are many books that give extensive histories of the Mediterranean diet including many facts and figures showing scientific findings and ranking the benefits of this diet in comparison to others, but as I said, the main purpose of this diet isn't to define it, but rather to help you achieve success once you've made the decision to adopt this lifestyle.

These are just a few of the many, many benefits of this diet. Plus, you as we have already said, this is more than a diet. This is a lifestyle. With this way of eating, you also are invited to adopt the Mediterranean approach to relaxation and recreation. Through the fuel and vitality you will derive from the food you are consuming you will have energy to live a an active lifestyle. Plus you many of these foods can cause a release of endorphins that will improve your mood and alleviate some of your stress allowing you to enjoy life more and not get as caught up In the details.

Indeed, a diet that encourages you to unwind with a glass of dry red wine at night can't be so bad.

## *What to Eat and What to Avoid:*

So what can you eat on the Mediterranean Diet? And What should you Avoid?

This is a diet of balance and moderation so there are very few types of foods that are absolutely forbidden. At most there are foods you should consume moderately or sparingly.

What you should eat a lot of:
- Fruits and veggies: almost all fruits and vegetables are fair game—so mix it up. The great thing about fruits and vegetables is that they're all so versatile and can be prepared in so many delicious and exciting ways that you'll never get bored.
    - Examples: broccoli, cauliflower, root vegetables (carrots, onions), greens (romaine, kale, spinach), tomatoes, eggplant, zucchini, cucumber, avocados, etc
    - Berries, apples, bananas, melons etc. (also dried fruits: dates, raisins, cranberries, cherries etc).

- Nuts: loaded with monounsaturated fats, they will leave you feeling satiated and full—with healthy fat.
    - Example: walnuts, almonds, hazelnuts, cashews, pumpkin seeds etc.
- Beans/Legumes: you will notice many of the recipes here include some form of legumes. Apart from introducing a lot of healthy fiber and protein, they will also help you feel full and stay full.
    - Garbanzo beans, white beans, black beans, lentils peas etc.
- Grains: any type of whole grain that is unadulterated and unrefined: oats, brown rice, whole wheat, quinoa, couscous etc.
- Fish: high in omega 3's as well as many other nutrients, most Americans do not consume nearly enough fish. This is a huge part of the Mediterranean diet:
    - Trout, tuna, shrimp, shellfish, salmon etc.
- Lean Meats: the better quality the better for you. Grass fed, organic lean beef chicken and pork are very welcome in the Mediterranean diet.
- Eggs and yogurt are great sources of protein and probiotics.
- Go crazy with herbs and spices, not only can they really enhance the flavor of your food, but they can enhance your health too (limit salt intake).

Generally, you'll want to avoid all processed sugars. Natural sugars like fruit are great, but keep the processed sugars to a minimum for best results.

Buy the best quality fruit you can find, and use it as a dessert replacement. If the fruit is actually good quality, you will get used to this new natural sweetness and it will instantly kill your sweet tooth.

# 7 Steps for Success in the Mediterranean Diet:

**1). Olive Oil:** you'll notice almost all of these recipes include olive oil. In moderation, olive oil has been shown to increase the good kind of cholesterol and it doesn't cause the negative health effects of processed oils and hydrogenated oils. In moderation, olive oil should be your monounsaturated fat of choice.

*make sure to buy extra virgin olive oil, and I recommend you invest in good quality olive oil not only for flavor, but chances are better that the vital nutrients are preserved in more authentic unprocessed olive oils.

**2). No Grain No Gain:** some diets instruct you to stay as far away from carbohydrates as possible. While we feel the same about processed and refined carbohydrates, whole grains are essential to the Mediterranean diet Avoid any type of "white" carbs (white bread, white rice, white pasta, white flour) as most of these types of carbs have been bleached and are now devoid of any beneficial nutrients and often contain harmful chemicals.

With wholegrains, you are consuming mostly unprocessed carbohydrates with their nutrients still intact. You will get the filling and satiating feeling from consuming carbohydrates while still benefitting from the nutrients.

**3). A glass of wine a day keeps the doctor away:**

For heart health, dry red wine in moderation is not only acceptable but encouraged in the Mediterranean diet. Places like Italy and Greece just wouldn't be the same if you had to give up wine, so let's be thankful for that. Limit yourself to a glass or half a glass per day. It's great way to unwind before bed.

**4). Fish are friends, also food:** as stated previously, most Americans do not eat enough fish. Apart from being a great source of quality protein with low levels of fat, most fish provide you with a healthy dose of omega-3 fatty acids (the good kind). Shop the sales, and don't be afraid to splurge a little for Salmon and Trout on occasion. See it as an investment in your health and treat yourself.

**5). Lean red meat in moderation:** Fatty red meat should be the exception and not the rule in the Mediterranean Diet. Leaner red meats especially lamb are fine in moderation, but fatty meats like beef ribs and steaks and burgers should be reserved for special occasions and otherwise avoided. But once you try a chargrilled salmon burger, or tuna steaks, you'll forget all about your burger.

**6). Beans are Best:** lentils, cannellini beans, garbanzo beans etc. are all very important to this diet. Try to get daily portions of legumes. I even like black beans or stewed lentils on my eggs in the morning. Not only are they a great source of fiber and protein, but they're low in fat, so you still feel very nice and full without loading up on fat.

**7). Pair the diet with an active lifestyle:** eating health is just one piece of the health puzzle (albeit one of the most important pieces). And since you'll be saving so much time by prepping your meals (with this book), you should have even more free time to pursue active leisure. The Mediterranean way isn't so much sweating buckets in the gym, but walking on a summer's night at sunset, or playing tennis with friends, or hiking in the foothills or riding a bike. Whatever your "active leisure" choose something you actually enjoy. Very few of us enjoy going to the gym, so choose something you'll actually look forward to doing in your free time. That way, you'll actually do it.

# Meal Prepping:

This book is all about meal prepping: one of the most important and often one of the most underrated tools in your arsenal for losing weight and staying committed to your diet.

Food prepping essentially is a way of cooking and mapping out your diet on a given week or set of days so that your meals are planned and prepared in advance as much as possible. This is absolutely essential for a busy person. You can confine all your cooking to just a few odd hours throughout your week, and still enjoy delicious and healthy home-cooked meals every day.

This book is a collection of Mediterranean Diet recipes that are specifically "prep-able." This means you will be able to prepare all or most of the dish in advance and spend minimal time preparing the dish before consumption the day of.

The reason this is so freeing for your life is that suddenly you are dieting and eating and cooking on your own terms. Instead of feeling like you have to spend every morning and night in the kitchen in order to stick to your diet, you are now able to base your cooking schedule around what is convenient for you and what fits best into your active lifestyle.

Maybe you have 1 or 2 prepping days a week, then the rest of the days require little to no time commitment in the kitchen. This means you suddenly have a lot more time on your hands AND you are much more likely to stick to your diet.

When you're coming home from a long day at work and facing the prospect of either cooking something for yourself or stopping in at your favorite restaurant or calling take out, you will be very tempted to choose one of the latter two options. The problem is that neither the restaurant nor the take out meals are probably in compliance with your dietary lifestyle. But if there's already a delicious healthy meal prepared and waiting for you, you'll find it much easier to resist temptation. Plus you will save money and be one step closer to your weight loss and health goals.

Meal prepping is the most effective strategy for managing your time effectively while still staying committed to your diet.

# 10 Tips to make you an Expert in Food Prepping:

**1) Choose Your Prepping Day In Advance**

This then becomes a part of your routine. We all have different regimens and commitments, but a Sunday can be a good day. Most people are not at work, and an hour or two can generally be found easily.

*Make it fun:* Find a good podcast, or put on your favorite music, and it can be great fun. You have the motivation of knowing that you are preparing food which will help you to achieve your end goals, be it weight loss, extra energy or just a better general fitness.

*Teamwork makes the dream work:* If a couple of you are on the diet in your household, working together can make it even more enjoyable. For instance, if you and your partner are on this dietary journey together, it can be a great bonding experience to prep together.

Pump up your favourite tunes, start chopping veggies, and portioning things out—not only are you ensuring you will stick to your diet that week, but you're spending quality time with your loved one and working together towards a common goal.

It will depend on your meal options, but it is possible that your dinners and lunches might not last until the end of the week. There are two ways of dealing with this. You could have a second, smaller prep time, perhaps on an evening where you know you will be in, or when it is usually a quiet day of work.

Another way is to plan your meals so that the longest lasting food is eaten at the end of the week. Later, we will give a detailed breakdown of how long various foods will survive in the fridge, both cooked and raw and offer advice on freezing as well. We will also give an indication of how long a meal will keep once prepared and, where appropriate, cooked. This information will be of great help as you plan your keto diet menu.

Choosing your prepping day can help you to establish a good routine. Just like with working out, the more you can set in place a plan, the less likely you'll be to deviate from it or fail to execute.

## 2) Plan Ahead

Not only does this apply to shopping, but also meal planning. When you go into your week with a plan, you will find you're much more successful in sticking to your diet than if you just try to wing it or make it up as you go.

Understanding the shelf life of ingredients is very important. Generally it's okay to stock up on non-perishables once a month, and fresh produce about twice per week. With the Mediterranean diet, you'll want to keep certain things on hand such as:

olive oil, dried fruits and nuts, canned foods such as artichokes, olives, beans, tuna etc and dried foods like beans, lentils, couscous, quinoa and whole grain pastas and brown rice.

Other foods you'll want to buy only after you've planned your menu for the week:

Fresh fruits, any type of green leaves, fresh vegetables, fresh meats, dairy, cheese, fresh fish etc.

Know the expiration date of these foods and make sure they are planned for use well before their expiration date.

Certain foods may need to ripen so if you buy them when they're unripe, you can buy them further in advance. A nice trick is to allow them to just sit out on your counter at room temperature until they're almost ripe, then refrigerate them until you're ready to use them. This helps prolong their shelf life and slow the ripening process if you're not ready to use those foods right away.

*A note on frozen foods:* frozen foods can be very helpful when it comes to meal prepping. Especially frozen vegetables, meats, fish and fruits. However, I strongly recommend using these sparingly. It isn't in keeping with the Mediterranean diet to use large quantities of frozen foods. Many studies have shown fruits and vegetables are lower in nutrients when frozen and then thawed. Wherever possible, try to use fresh produce in your cooking to more closely adhere to the essence of the Mediterranean diet.

### 3) Basic is Better:

As Socrates (a philosopher from the Mediterranean himself) said, "know thyself." Perhaps he wasn't speaking particularly about meal prepping, but we can pretend. Know yourself and be realistic with your expectations. As with any big life changes, start out small and basic and allow yourself to slowly work your way up to a larger scale change. If you are not used to cooking a lot for yourself, you may completely overwhelm yourself if you try to start cooking 3 meals a day all of the sudden. Start with just prepping one meal a day: I recommend starting with lunch.

If you're in the working world and end up eating out for most lunches, not only will your waist line thank you, but so will your wallet. In this book, I've focused on simple, realistic lunches that you can prep ahead easily a few times a week to save a lot of time and not have to worry about it the morning of when you're probably scrambling out the door to work.

Therefore, start small. Choose simple recipes that you know you will have time to make. Pick your prepping day ahead and block it off on your calendar so that you won't neglect it. You will be amazed at how quickly you will improve in time management, and before you know it, you'll be effortlessly prepping all your meals with time to spare.

**4) Invest in some good storage options:**

Of course plastic Tupperware is cheap, but it's probably the worst option for food storage. Not only are there many arguments that food storage in plastic can lead to chemical leaks and harmful health effects, but generally plastic containers are the worst at keeping your food fresh. You'll notice in the following chapters that I often recommend storing your food in glass.

Glass and metal containers are probably the best options both in terms of keeping your food fresh and not having to worry about chemicals. Plus the best part is, in glass containers you can heat the food up in the microwave directly without having to transfer to a plate. This can be a big help especially for your work lunches.

Otherwise, storing food on glass plates and wrapped in foil can be a good option also depending on the food. I've included specific information about this in the recipes section.

**5). Mason Jar Salads Rock:** just as you should invest in some good containers, you should definitely buy a set of mason jars as well. Layering a salad inside a mason jar makes one of the best, easiest packable lunches.

Not only does the glass jar keep your salad super fresh, but the way you layer it insures that it won't get soggy. Usually you'll keep the longer-lasting items such as meat, beans etc on the bottom with the dressing and do the items most likely to get soggy on top as far away from the dressing as possible (like spinach). Then when you're ready to eat, you just dump it out onto a plate and toss it. It's amazing. You'll wonder why you haven't been doing it this way all along.

One note on using mason jars to prep salads: any items you want to remain crunchy or crispy such as nuts should remain separate from the salad until you're ready to eat it. There's nothing worse than biting into a soggy lump when you're expecting a crunchy salty almond.

I'd recommend just storing the almonds you intend to use in the salad in a little plastic baggy at room temperature on the counter. Keep it in your desk at work and then when you get your salad out of the fridge, just top it with your almonds.

**6). The Freezer is your Friend:** I know I know what I said about using fresh vegetables and fruits, but there are circumstances where your freezer can be a great tool for you. Some of the dishes in this recipe book make great freezer meals. Let's face it, we all have those weeks where s*** hits the fan and no matter what we do we just don't have time to get everything done. If you have a few "emergency meals" saved in your freezer, problem solved. One less thing to worry about in your crazy week.

Additionally, there are certain foods where you can greatly prolong the shelf life by storing them in the freezer. One of my secrets is storing nuts in the freezer. Especially if you live in a humid area, your nuts can turn stale or get damp all too easily. And let's face it, nuts are EXPENSIVE, so the longer we can make those babies last, the better for our bank account.

*sale shopper not: if you're a sale shopper like me you might be tempted to buy a huge quantity of some food when they go on mega sale. That's where your freezer can help you. Buy in bulk at the sale price and freeze the excess for later use. Works like a charm.

## 7). When in doubt, slow cook it out:

Many meals can be adapted for the slow cooker. I've included several mouthwatering slow cooker recipes in this book and if you're already a slow cooker fan, you'll know what a life-saver these little machines are. Often times it really is as simple as "setting and forgetting." You just pile everything into the slow cooker and set the self-timer. This can be great for a busy person.

Throw everything into the slow cooker before bed and refrigerate then plug it in in the morning and set the timer for the indicated amount of time. You'll come home to a delicious hot meal waiting for you. Slow cooker creations are particularly tempting in the winter months when you have that itch for comfort food that you have to scratch.

**8). Make a grocery List:** I know this one is obvious, but you'd be amazed at how few people actually make grocery lists. There are 3 main benefits to having a grocery list:

- Save money: you will save money if you can make a list and stick to it. Grocery stores are notorious for luring you into buying all kinds of things you didn't intend to buy. If you don't go in with a plan, you'll end up filling your cart with things you may not even need. The store is even set up in such a way that distracts you with expensive items you didn't intend to buy. Your pocket will thank you if you make a list and get in and get out.
- Stick to your diet: similarly if you end up buying things that you didn't plan for or intend, it makes it very hard to stick to your diet. If you shop with no plan, old habits will return and you'll find yourself filling your cart with processed or sugary foods that have no business in your pantry or fridge. Make it easier for yourself by coming up with a plan of attack before stepping foot into the grocery store.
- Save time: there are two ways grocery lists save you time. The first way is during the actually shopping excursion. The times when I've shopped without a list, I spend most of the time aimlessly wandering around the store looking for inspiration of what to buy. If you already have that decision made for you, then all you have to do is go in, grab the items on your list and get out of there—mission accomplished. The other way it saves you time: if you don't have a list, good luck remembering everything you need for the recipes you'll be making that week. There's nothing worse than getting started preparing a dish only

> to find you're missing one of the key ingredients. Then you have to make an unplanned trip to the store—this eats away at your already precious free time.

Remember, the whole point of food prepping is to save you time, money and help you stick to your diet. Make a list and you're halfway there.

**9). Keep your menu fun and switch it up:** when you're trying to lose weight or improve your health, you do not want to get in a rut or get bored with your food. You want to be excited about your food and excited about the meals you've prepped. I think the recipes I've included in this book are pretty exciting and honestly you will feel like you're eating better than you did before your diet.

I recommend switching your menu up constantly though so you don't get sick of any one food. Even though there might be a few recipes you feel very confident with or that you could make in your sleep, venture out and keep trying new recipes.

The human mind and body responds best to variant inputs and we get tired of eating the same things over and over. The temptation will be to fall back on old habits. Or to treat yourself to take out or restaurant food when you're less than excited about the food that you prepare.

Therefore, it's very important to keep your menu bright and new and varied. Investing in cookbooks like this will really help you expand your recipe repertoire, and also there are many online communities with large recipe libraries. You will never run out of ideas—plus the more accustomed you get to this new way of eating and cooking, the more creative and innovative you will become. Who knows, maybe you'll come up with some new recipes of your own.

**10). Label Label and then Label some More:**
the whole reason you're meal prepping is to save time and take one more thing off your plate. The last thing you need is more things to keep track of. Don't leave it to your memory or to the sniff test whether or not you can/should use or eat something in your fridge. LABEL. Buy a sharpie and some masking tape.

All you have to do is put the "use by" date or at least the current day's date. This will help you prioritize how you use certain foods in your fridge and help you decide which leftovers to consume first. The result will be a lot less waste. And remember, wasted food also is wasted time. If food goes bad that just means more time you will have to spend preparing more food and going to the store to buy more food.

If you buy in bulk and freeze, you should definitely write the deets on the freezer bag. That way you can employ the last in-last out strategy to make sure you're consuming the oldest foods first.

Simple steps like these may seem obvious on paper, but just because we're trying to save time doesn't mean we should cut corners. In fact, employing these little strategies will help you save even more time and money in the long run.

# Some considerations regarding food prepping safety:

Of course meal prepping is completely safe, you just need to be educated and aware about the shelf life of certain foods and use common sense to avoid any contamination or sanitation issues.

- Keep raw meats away from other ingredients.
- Wash your hands, utensils and your spaces after touching any raw meats.
- Even if they are to be stored in sealed containers, raw meats should be stored at the bottom of the fridge, so they cannot drip onto other foods.
- Check the Use By' dates on food, and stick to them (especially with meat and dairy) produce you can be a little more lenient with especially if you are cooking it as opposed to eating it raw.
- Check the table for storage later in this book, and follow it closely.

*Make your own labels for the freezer and fridge to make sure you use food in time, saving waste and reducing the risk of food poisoning.*

- Complete the hand, surface and utensil washing procedures with raw vegetables as well as meats. Although less common, these can also contain bacteria as well as pesticides which can be harmful.
- Wash raw vegetables and fruit before consuming.

- Keep raw foods away from 'ready to eat' foods, such as salad or nuts, since you will not be washing these before consumption.
- If you are cooking food as a part of your prep, make sure that it is thoroughly cooked to avoid contamination.
- Check re-heating guidelines for foods. Some are fine, others, such as already frozen foods, are less safe.

As you can see, this is all common sense, but can be easily forgotten when you're in a rush.

- Do not wash raw meat – the water could spray around, spreading contamination.
- Do not re-freeze defrosted meat.
- Store meat separately, even cooked, if keeping for a while.
- After cooking, cool quickly and place in a sealed container in the fridge.
- When reheating, it needs at least two minutes at 70 degrees Celsius to be safe.
- If you are using defrosted meat, it must be consumed within twenty-four hours.

And now, onto the part you've been waiting for: the recipes!

# Part II: Recipes

# Breakfast/Brunch Recipes:

## *1). Tuscan Vegetable Frittata:*

6 eggs

1/3 cup milk

1 1/2 cups chopped spinach

1/2 cup diced sundried tomatoes

1/2 cup chopped black olives

1/4 cup crumbled feta Cheese

1 teaspoon Italian Seasoning

½ tsp. Olive Oil

Fresh Basil

**Instructions:**
1. Preheat oven to 400 degrees.
2. Pour ½ tsp Olive oil in a square baking pan or a deep pie plate
3. Whisk eggs and milk until well blended. Add sundried tomatoes, olives, Feta and Italian Seasoning. Mix slightly.
4. Bake for 15-20 minutes.
5. Top with more feta and fresh basil if desired.

**Prepping Instruction:** This makes 4 servings and can be stored in glass in the fridge for a few days. You can even slice it into pie-like slices and wrap in foil and take with you and heat up at work if it's a busy morning. Store in glass or foil for up to 3 days in the fridge.

**Yield:**

**Nutrition:** Calories: 177, Fat: 12g, Carbohydrates: 7.2g, Protein: 11.7g.

## 2). *Mediterranean Cranberry Breakfast Muffins:*

1 1/2 cups whole wheat flour

½ cups all purpose flour

1/4 cup sugar

2 tbps. honey

3 tsp baking powder

1 tsp. salt

1 c. dried cranberries

1 eggs

1/3 cup olive oil

1 cup 2% milk

Olive Oil Cooking Spray

**Instructions:**

1. Preheat oven to 400
2. In a Medium Mixing bowl, sift together wheat flour, all purpose flour, sugar, baking powder and salt.
3. In a separate bowl whisk together the honey, eggs, oil and milk
4. Make a well in the dry ingredients bowl and pour in the wet mixture. Mix with a spoon gently until just combined (do not overmix).
5. Grease muffin tins with olive oil cooking spray and distribute the batter across 1 dozen muffin cups. (You can also use paper muffin cups if desired)
6. Bake 15-17 minutes. Test with a toothpick. The muffins are done when the toothpick comes out clean.

**Prepping Instructions:** this recipe is great because it yields 12 small breakfasts which can last you over 2 work weeks. I suggest keeping the muffins in the freezer and just pop one in the microwave the morning of. This muffin and 2 eggs or a cup of unsweetened Greek yogurt make a great breakfast.

**Yield:** 12 muffins (12 servings)

**Nutrition:** Calories: 172, Fat: 6.6 g, Carbohydrates: 25.4 g, Protein: 3.3 g.

## *3). Slow Cooker Breakfast Quinoa with Blueberries:*

1 cup quinoa, dry

2 cups water

1 1/4 cup coconut milk divided

1 tablespoon honey

1 teaspoon vanilla extract

1/4 cup toasted almonds, sliced

1/2 cup fresh blueberries (or any fresh fruit desired)

**Instructions:**

1. Combine all ingredients except the almonds and blueberries and pour into the slow cooker.
2. Cook on low for 4 hours (or high for 2 hrs)
3. Top with a splash of coconut milk and toasted almonds and blueberries (I also like fresh peaches on top if they are in season)

**Prepping Instructions:** if your slow cooker has a timer, throw everything into the pot the night before and set it so that it starts 4 hours before you wake up. Then you'll have breakfast waiting for you when you wake up. Otherwise, just cook the night before and refrigerate. Heat in the microwave and eat. Store in glass for up to 3-4 days in the fridge.

**Yield:** 4 servings

**Nutrition:** Calories: 393, Fat: 23.5 g, Carbohydrates: 39.8 g, Protein: 9.1 g.

# *4). Greek Yogurt Parfait*

2 C. unsweetened greek yogurt

3/4 c. Wholegrain granola (unsweetened)

¼ c. dried dates, chopped

1/8 c. almonds toasted, slivered

4 tsp. honey

**Instructions:**

1. Put 1/4c. yogurt in the bottom of the jar or glass, then add a small amount of granola, another 1/4c. yogurt, a bit more granola, then top with dates, almonds and drizzle with 1tsp. honey

2. To keep the everything fresh, we recommend only assembling right before eating.

**Prepping Instructions:** just have the ingredients on hand and pre-measured. Then the morning of, you simply have to toss the ingredients together in a jar.

**Yield:** 4 servings

**Nutrition:** Calories: 404, Fat:19.4 g, Carbohydrates: 44 g, Protein: 18.2 g.

## 5). *Breakfast Polenta with Banana*

2 cups water

2 cups skim milk

1/4 teaspoon salt

1 cup instant or quick-cooking polenta

1/4 cup honey

½ cup sliced banana

Greek Yogurt (optional)

**Instructions:**

1. In a medium saucepan whisk together milk and water and salt and bring to a very gentle boil over medium-low heat. Whisk constantly so the milk doesn't scorch.

2. Pour in the instant polenta and whisk as the mixture thickens. Reduce the heat to low so the mixture is lightly simmering. Stir for 2-5 minutes and then remove from heat. Stir in the honey.
3. Allow to cool slightly
4. Spoon into bowls and top with banana slices (and dollop of Greek yogurt if desired)

**Prepping Instructions:** you can make this ahead, and then just heat in the microwave the morning of. Store in the fridge in glass for 3-4 days.

**Yield:** 4 servings

**Nutrition** (without Greek Yogurt): Calories: 154 Fat: 0 g, Carbohydrates: 33.7 g, Protein: 5 g.

## *6). Shakshukah Breakfast Skillet:*

2 tbsp. olive oil

1 Cup. Diced onion

1 bell pepper (orange, red or yellow)

2 cloves garlic, minced

1 teaspoon ground cumin

½ teaspoon kosher salt

¼ teaspoon ground black pepper

¼ tsp. Red pepper flakes (optional)

1 28 ounce can whole tomatoes

6 eggs

Feta cheese, crumbled

## Instructions:

1. Heat olive oil in a cast iron (or heavy bottomed skillet) over medium heat. Add the onion, bell pepper and garlic and all the spices and seasonings.
2. Stir making sure nothing gets burnt or sticks to the bottom of the pan. Sauté for 10 minutes.
3. Add the can of tomatoes (juice and all). Mix everything together and bring mixture to a gentle boil.
4. Simmer for another 10 minutes until the tomato juice starts to reduce and mixture thickens slightly.
5. Crack in the eggs one at a time. You may want to crack them into a small separate bowl first then add them to the dish that way you avoid any issues with shells or bad eggs.
6. Let the eggs sit in the sauce and cook until the eggs are cooked to your desired doneness.
7. Top with crumbled feta and serve.

**Prepping Instructions:** You can make the entire dish in advance and store in glass in the fridge for up to 3 days. Heat in the microwave or on the stove top and eat.

**Yield:** 4 servings

**Nutrition:** Calories: 278, Fat: 20 g, Carbohydrates: 12.5 g, Protein: 14.5 g.

## *8). Greek Omelet*

6 eggs

2 tbps. Whole milk

Fresh ground black Pepper

Kosher Salt

Italian Seasoning

1/4 c. canned/jarred artichoke harts chopped roughly

1/2 cup grape tomatoes, halved

1/4 sliced Kalamata olives

1/3 c. crumbled feta

1/2 c. prepared tzatziki sauce

Shredded fresh Basil (optional)

**Instructions:**

1. Vigorously whisk eggs milk salt and pepper and Italian seasoning. I like to use hand beaters to make the eggs really fluffy.
2. In a separate bowl, combine all the remaining ingredients.
3. Lightly grease a non-stick pan with olive oil cooking spray and pour in 1/4 the egg mixture.
4. Allow the egg mixture to set slightly as it cooks. Rotate the pan so the uncooked center part runs to the edges and spreads evenly. Once there is no more runniness, (about 1-2 minutes) remove from heat.
5. Add ¼ of the filling mixture to the bottom half of the flat omelet and then fold it in half
6. Repeat for the other 3 omelets.

**Prepping Instructions:**

You should make these fresh, the day of. The best way to prep is preparing everything ahead. You can even whisk the eggs mixture and store in a glass pitcher in the fridge. Combine all the fillings and store in a glass container in the fridge. The morning of, all you have to do is cook and assemble the omelet.

**Yield:** 4 Servings

**Nutrition:** Calories: 240 Fat: 18.5 g, Carbohydrates: 7.5 g, Protein: 12.8 g.

## 9). *Honey Walnut Overnight Oats:*

3 ½ cups of water

Pinch of salt

1 cup oats

½ tsp. vanilla extract

¼ c. honey

½ c. walnuts chopped

¼ c. pitted dates, chopped (or raisins if you prefer)

¼ c. milk

Instructions:
1. Bring water to a boil and toss in pinch of salt.
2. Then add the oats and give it a stir.
3. Turn off the heat, cover the pan and leave it sitting overnight.

**Prepping Instructions:** the morning of, just turn the oven back on and heat the oatmeal back up. Stir in the dates/raisins and honey. Top with a splash of milk and chopped walnuts.

**Yields:** 4 servings

**Nutrition:** Calories: 251, Fat: 11.4 g, Carbohydrates: 34.6 g, Protein: 5.5 g.

## *10). Mango Strawberry Breakfast Smoothie with Greek Yogurt*

1 banana

1 cup frozen strawberries

1 cup frozen mango

1 cup Greek yogurt

1/2 cup almond milk (or soy or cow)

1/4 tsp. ground cinnamon (optional)

**Instructions:**

1. Combine all ingredients in blender and pulse until smooth and completely blended.

**Prepping Instructions:** you can make this smoothie ahead and store in a glass jar in the fridge for up to 3 days.

**Yield:** 4 servings

**Nutrition:** Calories: 171, Fat: 8.4 g, Carbohydrates: 20, Protein: 6.4

# Lunch Recipes:

### *1). Mediterranean Quinoa Spinach Salad in a Jar*

1½ cup dry quinoa

½ teaspoon salt

Fresh ground pepper

1/3 cup olive oil

1 tablespoon red wine vinegar

2 garlic cloves, minced

½ teaspoon dry crushed basil

½ teaspoon dried crushed thyme

3 cups fresh greens of your choice (baby spinach, arugula etc)

1 15 oz can chickpeas

¼ c. black olives, sliced,

¼ c. roasted red peppers (from a jar) minced

Cherry Tomatoes (optional)

Fresh Basil (optional)

**Instructions:**

1. Cook quinoa following package directions
2. In a small bowl, mix together salt, pepper, oil, vinegar, basil, and thyme.
3. In the bottom of 4 mason jars, evenly portion out the chickpeas, olives, and red peppers. Then portion out the dressing you mixed together in the previous step pouring over the chickpeas
4. Add a layer of cooked quinoa (after it's cooled to room temperature), then last, top with the greens.
5. Seal Jar and store in the fridge

6. Top with tomatoes before eating if desired

**Prepping Instructions:** just keep the assembled salads in their jars in the fridge (store for up to 3-4 days). Shake and mix well before serving.

**Yield:** 4 servings

**Nutrition:** Calories: 446, Fat: 23 g, Carbohydrates: 51 g, Protein: 14 g.

## 2). Garbanzo Egg Salad with Honey Dijon Vinaigrette

1 15 oz can of chickpeas.

1 medium cucumber, chopped

½ c. red onion, sliced

6 large hard boiled eggs, sliced

2 c. spinach

1/2 cup chopped fresh basil

1/2 cup chopped fresh mint

*Dressing:*

2 1/2 tsp Dijon mustard

1 large lemon, zested and juiced

1/4 c. olive oil

2 tbsp. honey

½ tsp. garlic powder

½ tsp. Kosher salt

¼. Tsp. fresh ground black pepper

**Instructions:**
1. In a small bowl, combine all ingredients for dressing and whisk vigorously until mixed.
2. Mix together ingredients for salad and toss with dressing. (See prepping instructions).

**Prepping Instructions:** Pre-portion the salads into Tupperware for packable lunches. Keep the dressing separate. Portion out the spinach, then top with red onion, cucumber, egg, chickpeas and herbs. Only toss with dressing right before eating. Store salads in air tight tuperware for 3-4 days in the fridge. Shake dressing well before tossing the salad.

**Yield:** 4 servings

**Nutrition:** Calories: 120, Fat: 21 g, Carbohydrates: 36 g, Protein: 16.7

## *3). Tuna Salad Avocado Boats*

2 (6oz) cans of Tuna

4 tbsp. Olive oil Mayo

¼ c. red onion, chopped

2 Stalks of Celery, chopped small

1 tsp. Balsamic vinegar

Salt and Pepper

2 medium avocados

**Instructions:**

1. Drain the tuna and combine in a small bowl with all other ingredients except avocado.
2. When ready to serve, halve the avocado, remove the pit and stuff ¼ of the tuna mixture into the center. Garnish with more red onion and tomato slices if desired

**Prepping Instructions:** do not cut the avocado until you're ready to eat. Proportion the tuna salad into 4 small containers. The morning of, slice the avocado and squeeze lemon juice on it to keep it from turning brown. Bring the avocado half and the tuna to work with you and assemble before eating. The tuna mixture can keep up to 3-4 days in glass in the fridge.

**Yield:** 4 servings

**Nutrition:** Calories: 305, Fat: 20 g, Carbohydrates: 8 g, Protein: 23 g.

## *4). Classic Greek Salad in a Jar*

1 can (15 oz) chickpeas

1 large cucumber, chopped

½ c. black olives sliced

2 Roma tomatoes, diced

1/4 cup red onion, sliced

3 tablespoons olive oil

1 tablespoon lemon juice

1/4 teaspoon salt

1/8 teaspoon pepper

5 cups torn mixed salad greens

1/2 cup crumbled feta cheese

**Instructions:**
1. Whisk together the lemon, oil, salt and pepper in a small bowl.
2. Drain and rinse the chickpeas and portion out into 4 medium sized mason jars. Pour the olive oil mixture over the beans.
3. Then add the olives, cucumber, tomato and onion.
4. Then add the greens and top with Feta.

**Prepping Instructions:** Store the jars in the fridge for up to 4 days. Shake well and toss before eating

**Yield:** 4 servings

**Nutrition:** Calories: 324 g, Fat: 17.7 g, Carbohydrates: 36 g, Protein: 12 g.

## 5). *Pork Loin and Orzo:*

1 pound pork tenderloin

1 teaspoon coarsely ground pepper

1 tsp. kosher salt

2 tablespoons olive oil

1 cups uncooked orzo pasta

Water

2 cups spinach

1 cup cherry tomatoes, halved

3/4 cup crumbled feta cheese

**Instructions:**

1. Coat the pork loin with the kosher salt and black pepper and massage it into the meat. Then cut the meat into one-inch cubes.
2. Heat the olive oil in a cast iron skillet over medium heat until sizzling hot. Cook the pork for about 8 minutes until there's no pink left.
3. Cook the orzo in water according to package directions (adding a pinch of salt to the water).
4. Stir in the spinach and tomatoes and add the cooked pork. Top with feta.

**Prepping Instructions:** Prepare ahead of time and store fully assembled in glass up to 3 days. Enjoy cold or heat up in the microwave or on the stovetop if desired.

**Yield:** 4 servings

**Nutrition:** Calories: 385, Fat: 17.4 g, Carbohydrate: 18.9 g, Protein: 37 g.

# *6). Tuna and White Bean Lettuce Wraps*

8 Bibb lettuce leaves

12 oz. canned tuna, drained

1 (15oz) can cannellini beans, rinsed and drained

1/4 cup red onion, chopped

1/2 c. corn

2 tablespoons balsamic vinegar

2 tablespoons olive oil

1 tablespoon minced fresh basil

1/8 teaspoon pepper

1/8 teaspoon salt

1 medium ripe avocado, pitted, peeled and diced

**Instructions:**
1. Wash bibb lettuce leaves. Pat dry with paper towels or use salad spinner until leaves are as dry as possible.
2. In a bowl combine all the remaining ingredients. Portion out the tuna mixture into 4 tupperware containers.
3. Before eating, spoon 1/8 of the tuna mixture into a lettuce leaf and tuck in the edges.

**Prepping Instructions:** Store the tuna mixture in Tupperware in the fridge for up to 3 days. Keep the lettuce leaves separate. Assemble before eating.

**Yield:** 4 servings

**Nutrition:** Calories: 334, Fat: 19.7 g, Carbohydrates: 18.2 g, Protein: 24.8 g.

# 7). Warm Tuscan Artichoke Salad

3 cloves garlic, minced

1 tablespoon extra virgin Olive oil

1 small red onion, sliced

1 can crushed tomatoes

18 oz frozen artichokes,

1 tablespoon Fresh lemon juice

1/2 c. white wine

Salt and Fresh Black Pepper

1/3 c. freshly grated parmesan

Sundried Tomatoes (for garnish

**Instructions:**
1. In a medium skillet, heat the olive oil. Add the onion and start to saute and stir until the onions start to soften. Add the garlic stirring frequently to keep the garlic from sticking to the bottom of the pan.
2. Add the wine and cook until the wine is reduced to about half the original amount.
3. Add the canned tomatoes, artichokes, lemon juice, salt and pepper to taste.
4. Top with parmesan and sundried tomatoes

**Prepping Instructions:** store in glass and keep in the fridge for up to 4 days. Heat in the microwave before eating.

**Yield:** 4 servings

**Nutrition:** Calories: 222, Fat: 10.2 g, Carbohydrates: 17.8 g, Protein: 13.9 g.

## 8). Roasted Zucchini with Yogurt and Dill

2 tablespoons extra virgin olive oil

1 lb. Zucchini, peeled and chopped into 1 inch cubes

1/2 vidalia (sweet) onion, sliced roughly

4 cloves garlic, minced

1/2 tsp. kosher salt

1/4 tsp. Black pepper

1/4 cup slivered almonds

Kosher salt and Black Pepper

2/3 cup greek yogurt

1 1/2 Tablespoons fresh dill

**Instructions:**
1. Preheat the oven to 400 degrees.
2. Toss the zucchini cubes in the olive oil with the garlic, onion, salt and pepper. Roast on a baking sheet for 25-30 minutes
3. Allow to cool slightly and then toss the roasted vegetables in the Greek yogurt. Top with almonds and fresh dill.

**Prepping:** prepare all the ingredients but wait and roast the vegetables right before eating. Store in a plastic ziplock. Only roast and top with yogurt and dill and almonds only right before eating.

**Yield:** 4 servings

**Nutrition:** Calories: 143, Fat: 10 g, Carbohydrates: 8 g, Protein: 7.4 g.

# 9). Roasted Red Pepper Hummus with Fresh Veggies

1 (15oz) can of chickpeas

1/4 cup tahini

2 tablespoons extra virgin olive oil

1/4 cup fresh squeezed lemon juice

2 cloves garlic, minced

2 tablespoons extra virgin olive oil

1/2 teaspoon ground cumin

3/4 cup fire roasted red peppers (from the jar)

Pinch cayenne pepper (optional)

Assorted vegetables: (cauliflower and broccoli florets, snow peas, carrot sticks, celery etc).

**Instructions:**
1. Combine all ingredients in the food processor and pulse until desired consistency
2. Serve with raw vegetables

**Prepping Instructions:** Store in glass for up to a week and serve with vegetables.

**Nutrition per 2 Tablespoons** (Not including vegetables): Calories: 50, Fat: 3.5 g, Carbohydrates: 4 g, Protein: 1 g.

## *10). Greek Tacos:*

2 medium chicken breasts, cooked and shredded

4 Cups chopped lettuce (Romaine or other preferred)

1 Cup halved cherry tomatoes (red and yellow for color)

3/4th Cup Diced Cucumbers

2 tbsp. fresh mint, chopped

1 Cup Feta Cheese Crumbled

1/2 Cup Sliced Black Olives

¼ c. olive oil

¼ c. balsamic vinegar

½ tsp. kosher salt

¼ tsp. black pepper

1/3 Cucumber and Dill Grek Yogurt Dip

8 whole grain small tortillas or low carb mini wraps

**Instructions:**
1. Toss together the shredded chicken, tomato, cucumber, olives and and mint. Add the oil and vinegar salt and pepper and mix.
2. To build the tacos, scoop 1/8$^{th}$ of the chicken mixture into each tortilla, add the lettuce, and feta, and top with a dollop of Greek yogurt dip

**Prepping Instructions:** Keep the chicken mixture in a glass container in the fridge — separate from the lettuce and tortillas. Store for up to 3 days. Assemble the tacos the morning of right before work or right before lunch if possible and wrap in waxed paper and keep refrigerated until you're ready to eat.

**Yield:** 4 servings (8 tacos)

**Nutrition: Calories:** 424, Fat: 28.3 g, Carbohydrates: 17.8 g, Protein: 33.1 g.

## 11). Turkey Lentil Meatballs with Tzatziki Dipping Sauce

1 lb lean ground turkey

1 cup cooked brown lentils

2 eggs

½ c. panko breadcrumbs

¼ c. grated parmesan

1/4 cup crumbled feta cheese

2 clove garlic, minced

2 tablespoons red onion, minced very fine

2 tablespoon capers

1 tablespoon Greek Seasoning

1 teaspoon kosher salt

1/2 teaspoon ground black pepper

1 cup Tzatziki Dipping Sauce, prepared

**Instructions:**

1. Put the cooked lentils in a blender and pulse until they are completely broken down
2. Combine all ingredients except for the tzatziki in a large bowl and mix well. Use your hands to fully incorporate all ingredients.
3. Separate into 20 balls and roll them until they are even and round.
4. Cook on a greased cookie sheet at 375 for 20 minutes (or until fully cooked). You can check with a meat thermometer if you're unsure.
5. Serve with Tzatziki dipping sauce and fresh lemon.

**Prepping Instructions:** refrigerate up to 3 days or freeze for use any time. Heat in microwave in a glass dish with a tablespoon of water. Each serving is 5 meatballs with ¼ cup of Tzatziki. Squeeze fresh lemon on top if desired.

**Yield:** 4 servings (about 5 meatballs each serving)

**Nutrition:** Calories: 394, Fat: 19.6 g, Carbohydrates: 17.8 g, Protein: 40.9 g.

## *12). Chilled Artichoke Zucchini Salad*

2 medium Chicken Breasts, cooked and cut into 1 inch cubes

1/4 c. Extra Virgin Olive Oil

2 c. artichoke hearts (drained from a jar), roughly chopped

3 Large Zucchini, diced or cut into small rounds

1 (15oz) can of Chickpeas

1 c. Kalamata Olives

½ tsp. Fresh ground black Pepper

½ tsp. Italian Seasoning

¼ cup. Grated Parmesan

**Instructions:**

1. Heat the olive oil in a large skillet and saute Zucchini until it starts to soften (about 5 minutes). Add salt and pepper and stir.
2. Remove from heat and mix all ingredients in the skillet until well combined.
3. Transfer to a glass container and store in the fridge. Serve cold

**Prepping Instructions:** Keep in glass in the fridge for up to 3 days. Serve cold (or pre-portion into 4 Tupperware for 4 work lunches.

**Yield:** 4 Servings

**Nutrition:** Calories: 457, Fat: 22.7 g, Carbohydrates: 30.1 g, Protein: 30.6 g.

## 13). White Bean Soup

2 cups shredded chicken (yield from a whole chicken cooked and bones/skin removed)

1 large carrot, sliced into rounds

1 large leek, sliced into rounds

2 tsp. Extra Virgin Olive Oil

½ tsp. sage

½ tsp. Italian Seasoning

Salt and Pepper

28 oz. Chicken Broth

1 (15 oz) can of Cannellini Beans

2 c. Water

**Instructions:**
1. Heat oil in a large pot and salute leeks and carrots until they become tender (about 4 minutes).
2. Add seasonings and salt and pepper and stir and cook for 1 minute longer.
3. Add all remaining ingredients and stir until well combined.
4. Cook until flavor is to your desired taste.

**Prepping Instructions:** Store in glass in the fridge for up to 3 days. Heat on the stove top or in the microwave before eating.

**Yield:** 4 servings

**Nutrition:** Calories: 281, Fat: 6.8 g, Carbohydrates: 22.8 g, Protein: 30.8 g.

## 14). Balsamic Beet Salad with Blue Cheese and Walnuts

3 cups canned beets, drained

1/4 cup red wine vinegar

¼ cup balsamic vinegar

2 tablespoon olive oil

½ tsp. kosher salt

½ tsp. fresh ground black pepper

8 cups fresh spinach

1/4 cup chopped apple

Freshly ground pepper

4 tablespoons chopped walnuts

1/4 cup blue cheese (or feta if you prefer), crumbled

Fresh Parsley or mint, For Garnish

**Instructions:**
1. In a small bowl, whisk together vinegars, oil, salt and pepper.
2. In another bowl, toss together all remaining ingredients.
3. Only dress the salad right before eating. Top with fresh herbs for garnish and extra flavor.

**Prepping Instructions:** store the salad in metal or glass in the fridge for up to 2 days. Keep the dressing separate and only toss the salad when you're ready to eat. (you may also want to keep the walnuts separate until you're ready to eat so they stay crunchy).

**Yield:** 4 servings

**Nutrition:** Calories: 225, Fat: 14.5 g, Fat: 20.1 g, Protein: 7.5 g.

## 15) Lebanese Tabbouleh

1 cup firm tomatoes, chopped small

1/2 cup bulgur wheat

1 medium cucumber, diced small

2 cups loosely packed Italian Parsley, stems removed, chopped

1/4 cup chopped fresh mint

1/3 cup green onion, chopped small

Kosher salt and black pepper

¼ c. freshly squeezed Lemon Juice

¼ c. Extra virgin Olive Oil

Baby Spinach (optional)

**Instructions:**
1. Put the bulgar wheat in a small bowl and cover with water. Soak for 5-6 minutes, drain off the water, and put the wheat in a kitchen towel and squeeze out any excess water
2. Combine all ingredients in a large bowl mixing well and seasoning with salt and pepper to taste. Allow to chill at least 30 minutes before serving. (Note: make sure the vegetables and herbs are chopped very fine for best results).

**Prepping Instructions:** you can reserve the lemon juice and oil until the day of consumption. Without the oil and lemon, you can store the salad in glass for up to 3 days in the fridge. Add the oil and lemon and mix well before eating.

**Yield:** 4 servings

**Nutrition:** Calories: 207, Fat: 14.4 g, Carbohydrate: 21.7 g, Protein: 4.4 g.

# Dinner Recipes:

## *1). Stuffed Peppers:*

2 tsp. Extra virgin olive oil

6 bell peppers, tops removed, seeds scooped out

1 onion, chopped

1 cup garbanzo beans

1/2 lb ground beef

1/2 tsp garlic powder

1 tsp. Kosher salt

1/4 tsp. Fresh ground black pepper

1/2 cup chopped parsley

1 tsp. Italian seasoning

2 cups cooked whole grain rice (brown rice or whatever your preference)

¼ tsp. cayenne pepper

1 (15 oz. Can of tomato Sauce)

**Instructions:**
1. In a skillet, heat the olive oil over medium heat. Sauté onions until they're soft 3-5 minutes. Add the ground beef and cook until there's no pink breaking the beef up until crumbly with a spatula.
2. Transfer to a bowl and add all remaining ingredients except for tomato sauce and Bell peppers.

3. Mix until well combined, then portion out the meat/rice mixture into the 6 bell peppers.
4. Place the peppers into the slow cooker and pour the tomato sauce evenly over the stuffed peppers.
5. Cook on low for 6 hours.

**Prepping Instructions:** store in glass up to 3 days in the fridge. Heat in the microwave. You can prep this dish the night before and set your slow cooker to cook during the day so you'll have a hot meal waiting for you when you get home for dinner.

**Yield:** 4 Servings:

**Nutrition:** Calories: 453, Fat: 10 g, Carbohydrates: 63 g, Protein: 33 g.

## 2). *Slow Cooker Pork Tenderloin with Mediterranean Quinoa Salad*

¼ c. extra virgin olive oil

½ tsp. kosher salt

¼ tsp. freshly ground black pepper

1.5 lbs of pork tenderloin

1 cup chicken broth

4 garlic cloves, minced very fine

Salt and pepper

1 cup quinoa

2 tablespoons apple cider vinegar

1/2 cup minced fresh parsley

1/2 cup dried cranberries

1/2 cup sliced almonds, toasted

**Instructions:**
1. Pour the chicken broth into the bottom of the slow cooker pan.
2. Season and pat the pork tenderloin with salt, pepper and half of the garlic then transfer into the slow cooker.
3. Cook about 2 hours on low or until meet thermometer reads 160 degrees. Then pull the pork out of the slow cooker and place it on a cutting board.
4. Pour the liquid in the slow cooker into a liquid measuring cup and pour back into the slow cooker 1 cup of the liquid. Add in the quinoa and cook on high for around 15 minutes or until the quinoa is cooked and fluffy. Add the cranberries and almonds and mix.
5. I a small bowl, whisk together oil, vinegar, ½ tsp. salt, and ¼ tsp. pepper, the rest of the garlic and the parsley. Whisk until the vinaigrette is well combined.
6. Slice the tenderloin and serve with the quinoa. Drizzle the vinaigrette over both.

**Prepping instructions:** this entire meal can be made in advance and reheated. Keep the vinaigrette separate and only pour over the food when you're ready to eat. Store quinoa and pork separately in glass for up to 3 days in the fridge. Re heat in the microwave or in the slow cooker.

**Yield:** 4 servings

**Nutrition:** Calories: 564, Fat: 24.5 g, Carbohydrates: 30.9 g, Protein: 53.4 g.

## *3). Spinach Pasta Fazool*

1 tablespoon olive oil

½ tsp. kosher salt

¼ tsp. black pepper

¼ tsp. Cayenne pepper (optional)

1 onion, chopped

1 large tomato, diced

2 stalks celery, chopped

chopped 3 cloves garlic

2 teaspoon Italian seasoning

2 Tablespoons fresh parsley, chopped

2 cups chicken broth

1 cup tomato sauce

1/2 cup spinach pasta, uncooked

1 (15 oz) can cannellini beans

**Instructions:**
1. In a medium skillet, heat oil and saute onion, celery and garlic. Add salt, pepper, cayenne, Italian seasoning, and parsley. Continue sauteeing over medium heat until onions are soft and tender (5-7 minutes).
2. Add the chicken broth and tomato stirring. Reduce heat slightly and simmer for 20 minutes.
3. Add the uncooked pasta and cook for 10 minutes or until the pasta reaches your desired doneness.
4. Remove from heat, and stir in the beans (including the liquid). Garnish with fresh parmesan if desired.

**Prepping Instructions:** store in glass up to 4 days in the fridge. Serve hot or cold — whatever you prefer.

**Yield:** 4 Servings

**Nutrition**: Calories: 276 g, Fat: 7 g, Carbohydrates: 41 g, Protein: 13 g.

## *4). Zesty Lentil Zuppa Toscana*

2 tsp. Extra virgin olive oil

2 cloves garlic, minced

1 large onion

½ tsp kosher salt

1 1/2 tsp crushed red pepper flakes

¼ tsp. fresh ground black pepper

1 tsp ground cumin

1/4 c. fresh mint, chopped

1 tbsp flour

¼ tsp. sugar

3 cups Water

6 cups chicken broth (or vegetable if desired)

2 (6oz) packages of frozen spinach

1 cup parsley, chopped

1 1/2 cups lentils, uncooked

1 tablespoon lemon juice

**Instructions:**
1. In a medium skillet, heat the oil and salute the onions for about 5 minutes until they begin to soften. Add the garlic and all the herbs and spices including the mint, flour and sugar and stir continuing to sauté for 1-2 minutes more or until the garlic is fragrant.
2. Add the broth and water and bring the soup to a full boil. Next add the frozen spinach and the lentils. Keep the soup boiling on high for 5 minutes stirring.
3. Reduce the heat to low and simmer for 20 minutes.
4. Once the lentils are fully cooked, remove from heat and stir in the lemon juice and the parsley.

**Prepping Instructions:** store up to 4 days in the fridge (or freeze for use later). Heat up on the stove top for best results. (Microwave is okay if the soup is refrigerated, but I do not recommend using the microwave for thawing the frozen soup).

**Yield:** 4 Servings

**Nutrition:** Calories: 389, Fat: 6.1g, Carbohydrates: 51.6 g, Protein: 29.6 g.

## 5). Pan Seared Eggplant Medallions with Balsamic Reduction

1 cup balsamic vinegar

2 tbsp. honey

1/2 tsp. kosher salt

¼ tsp. fresh ground black pepper

2 tbsp extra virgin olive oil

3 medium, or 2 large eggplants, sliced into ½ inch rounds

2 tbsp. fresh mint, chopped

4 eggs

Instructions:
1. In a small saucepan, heat the balsamic vinegar and stir in the honey. Whisk regularly as you bring it to a boil. Then reduce

heat and simmer for 20 minutes as the vinegar reduces and starts to thicken.
2. Heat the olive oil in a large cast iron skillet. Sear the eggplant rounds for 3-4 minutes on both sides. Season with salt and pepper.
3. In another nonstick skillet coated with olive oil cooking spray, fry the eggs to desired doneness.
4. Portion out the eggplant onto 4 plates and place a fried egg on top of each portion of eggplant. Drizzle with Balsamic reduction and top with fresh mint and serve.

**Prepping Instructions:** You can slice the eggplant, and make the balsamic sauce ahead. Just before eating, fry the eggplant and eggs and put everything together before eating.

**Yield:** 4 servings

**Nutrition:** Calories: 272, Fat: 12 g, Carbohydrates: 34 g, Protein: 9.7 g.

## *6). Oven Roasted Garlic Chicken Thighs*

8 chicken thighs

salt and pepper

1 Tbsp extra virgin olive oil

6 cloves garlic, peeled and crushed

1 10 oz. jar roasted red peppers, drained and chopped up

1 1/2 pounds potatoes, diced small

2 c. cherry tomatoes, halved

1/3 cup capers (or green olives sliced if you don't have capers)

1 tsp dried Italian Seasoning

1 tablespoon fresh basil

**Instructions:**

1. Season the chicken with kosher salt and black pepper
2. Sear the chicken in the hot olive oil in a cast iron skillet over medium-high heat until golden on both sides.
3. Add the remaining ingredients except for basil and stir.
4. Remove from the heat and place the cast iron skillet in the oven—or transfer to an oven safe pan if you're not using a cast iron or oven safe skillet.
5. Bake at 400 for 45 minutes or until meat thermometer reads 165 degrees.

**Prepping Instructions:** Wrap in foil and store for up to 3 days in the fridge. Heat in the microwave with a teaspoon of water to keep it moist.

**Yield:** 4 servings

**Nutrition:** Calories: 500, Fat: 23 g, Carbohydrates: 37 g, Protein: 35 g.

## *7). Roasted Carrot Ginger Bisque*

2 tbsp. extra virgin olive oil

Kosher Salt and Fresh Ground Black Pepper

3 lb. carrots, peeled

4 cloves garlic, minced

2 inches fresh ginger root, peeled and grated

5 cups vegetable stock

1 tsp allspice

2 tsp. fresh cilantro, chopped

1 cup milk

½ cup greek Yogurt

**Instructions:**

1. Drizzle carrots with olive oil and season with a generous amount of salt and pepper tossing to coat the carrots with oil and spices.
2. Roast the carrots on a cookie sheet at 425 degrees for about 40-50 minutes or until the carrots are completely tender and caramelized. You'll want to flip the carrots over about 25 minutes into cooking. Remove the carrots from the oven and allow them to cool slightly.
3. Chop the roasted carrots into cubes and throw them in the food processor. Add the garlic, broth and ginger and pulse until the whole mixture is smooth and there are no chunks.
4. Pour into a cooking pot. Add the cilantro and allspice and stir over medium heat allowing the mixture to simmer.
5. Continue cooking for 10 minutes simmering lightly.
6. Turn the heat all the way down to low and stir in the milk and yogurt. Remove from the stove and serve with fresh parsley if desired.

**Prepping Instructions:** store in the fridge in a glass or metal container for up to 4 days. Heat on the stovetop for best results.

**Yield:** 4 servings

**Nutrition:** Calories: 258, Fat: 8.9 g, Carbohydrates: 39.5 g, Protein: 7.6 g.

## 8). Garlic Lentil Bowls

1 tablespoon extra-virgin olive oil

6 cloves garlic, minced

2 onions, diced

2 cups dried lentils, rinsed

1 teaspoon kosher salt

1/2 teaspoon paprika

1/4 teaspoon pepper

1/2 teaspoon ground ginger

3 cups vegetable broth

3/4 cup Greek yogurt

1/4 cup lemon juice

3 tablespoons tomato paste

**Instruction:**
1. Heat the oil in a pot and saute the onions at medium heat for 4-5 minutes until the onions start to soften and brown at the edges. Add the garlic and stir for about 2 minutes.
2. Add the lentils and pour in the vegetable broth. Bring to a boil, then reduce heat and simmer for 30 minutes or until the lentils are fully cooked and tender.
3. Stir in all remaining ingredients and serve.

**Prepping:** store in a glass container for up to 3 days in the fridge. Enjoy cold or heat in the microwave before eating.

**Yield:** 4 servings

**Nutrition:** Calories: 470, Fat: 6 g, Carbohydrates: 29 g, Protein: 34.3 g.

## 9). *Balsamic Chicken Skewers with Summer Vegetables*

1/4 cup balsamic vinaigrette

1/4 cup barbecue sauce

1 teaspoon Dijon mustard

1-1/2 lbs chicken breast, cut into 1 inch cubes and seasoned with salt and pepper

2 cups cherry tomatoes

2 bell peppers chopped into large chunks

1. large zucchini chopped into rounds

## Instructions:

1. Soak the skewers in water for a few minutes
2. In a small bowl, whisk together, the BBQ sauce, Dijon Mustard, and Balsamic Vinaigrette. Set aside a small amount for dipping later.
3. Marinate the chicken cubes in this sauce and mix to coat the chicken cubes.
4. Load the skewers with the vegetables and chicken alternating
5. Grill for several minutes on each side until the chicken is fully cooked and vegetables get grill marks.
6. Serve with the extra sauce that did not touch the raw chicken.

**Prepping Instructions:** make the skewers and store in the fridge on plates with foil for up to 2 days. Grill before eating.

**Yield:** 4 servings

**Nutrition:** Calories: 255, Fat: 9.4 g, Carbohydrates: 15.7 g, Protein: 26.4 g.

## *10). Caprese Stuffed Chicken*

2 lbs boneless skinless chicken breast

2 tablespoons olive oil

Kosher Salt and Fresh Cracked Pepper

½ teaspoon garlic powder

½ cup of balsamic vinegar

1 tablespoon honey

8 oz. fresh mozzarella, cut into even slices

1 cup halved cherry tomatoes

⅓ cup fresh sliced basil

**Instructions:**

1. Season the chicken breast with salt pepper and garlic powder.

2. Heat the oil in a large skillet. When the oil is hot, sear the chicken and continue to cook 5-8 minutes on each side until meat thermometer reads 165 degrees.
3. Remove the chicken from the pan and allow to rest on a cutting board.
4. Pour the vinegar and honey into the pan and simmer until the mixture starts to thicken and reduce. Remove from heat.
5. When the chicken has cooled slightly, slice each breast in half (lengthwise) so there is a top and bottom.
6. Layer tomato slices, basil and mozzarella on the bottom chicken half and place the top on. Drizzle with balsamic reduction and serve with more fresh basil for garnish if desired. If you want the cheese to be melted, place the chicken under the broiler for a few minutes.

**Prepping Instructions:** Cook the chicken and keep it separate from the other ingredients. Keep refrigerated for up to 3 days. Assemble the Caprese Chicken right before eating.

**Yield:** 4 servings

**Nutrition:** Calories: 536, Fat: 24 g, Carbohydrates: 9 g, Protein: 44 g.

## *11). Mediterranean Quinoa Bake*

1 large onion, diced

4 cloves garlic, minced

2-1/2 cups cooked cup quinoa

1-1/2 cups cooked brown lentils

2 tablespoons extra virgin olive oil

2-3 cups of fresh baby spinach

1 cup cherry tomatoes, halved

2 eggs

1/2 cup Greek yogurt

½ c. crumbled feta

1/2 teaspoon salt

¼ tsp. Black Pepper

2 tsp. Dried Dill

**Instructions:**

1. Heat oil in a medium skillet. Saute onions for 3 minutes then add the garlic and continue stirring and sautéing for about 2 more minutes until the garlic is fragrant and the onions are tender.
2. Add the spinach and reduce the heat slightly. Stir and cover the pan for about 5-7 minutes until the spinach is completely wilted. Remove from heat and stir in lentils and tomatoes
3. In a separate bowl, mix yogurt, eggs, feta, salt, pepper and dill. Stir in the quinoa.
4. Combine the yogurt mixture and spinach lentil mixture and mix until everything is well incorporated, then pour the mixture into a greased square baking dish.
5. Bake at 375 for about 30-40 minutes or until the top is golden and slightly bubbly.

**Prepping Instructions:** there are 3 options here: cook the casserole and store in the fridge for up to 4 days, or freeze, thaw and heat up whenever you need a quick meal fix. Otherwise, you can prepare the dish and pour it into the pan but don't bake it yet. Cover the pan with foil and store in the fridge for up to 2-3 days. Bake when you're ready to eat.

**Yield:** 4 servings

**Nutrition:** Calories: 345, Fat: 16 g, Carbohydrates: 38 g, Protein: 17.8 g.

## *12). Slow Cooker Honey Garlic Chicken Thighs*

1 tablespoon honey

1/3 cup white wine

1-1/2 tsp. Italian Seasoning

1/4 cup red wine vinegar

Kosher salt and Black pepper

4 cloves garlic, minced

1/3 cup green olives, sliced

8 small chicken thighs

¼ cup fresh flat-leaf parsley, chopped

**Instructions:**

1. Combine all ingredients except for the parsley and chicken thighs in the pan of the slow cooker.
2. Then place the chicken in the slow cooker and cover. Cook on high for 6 hours on low or 3-4 hrs on high.
3. Before servings, add the parsley and stir

**Prepping Instructions:** Store in glass or stoneware and keep refrigerated for up to 3 days. Heat in the oven or microwave before eating.

## *13). Spaghetti Squash and Meatballs*

1 tbsp. extra virgin olive oil

1 large Spaghetti Squash

1 (14.5 oz) jars of fire roasted diced tomatoes

2 c. Pomodoro sauce (plain marinara)

4 cloves garlic, minced

1 large yellow onion, diced

2 tsp. dried Italian seasoning

1 tsp. dried basil

1/2 tsp. dried oregano

Kosher salt and fresh black pepper to taste

1/4 tsp. fennel seeds (optional)

Red pepper flakes (optional)

20 frozen meatballs

1/4 c. fresh grated parmesan cheese

**Instructions:**

1. In a skillet over medium heat, heat the olive oil. Sauté the onions for 5 minutes, then add the garlic and cook for 2 more minutes stirring. Make sure nothing is sticking to the bottom of the pan. Add the fire roasted tomatoes, the pomodoro and all the herbs and spices. Stir until everything is incorporated and reduce heat to medium low, leave for 15 minutes with the lid propped.

2. Cut the spaghetti squash in half and remove the seeds and the stringy pulp (be careful not to remove the flesh of the squash). Place cut-side down in the slow cooker.
3. Pour the tomato sauce from the skillet into the slow cooker, over the squash. Arrange the meatballs in the sauce around the squash and make sure the meatballs are all covered in sauce.
4. Cook on low for 7-8 hours or high for 3-4.
5. Remove the spaghetti squash. Scoop out the spaghetti squash with fork and it will come apart in spaghetti-like strings.
6. Top with grated parmesan.

**Prepping Instructions:** store in glass and keep spaghetti, sauce and meatballs separate and portion out and heat only before eating. Store for up to 3 days

**Yield:** 4-5 servings

**Nutrition per Serving:** Calories: 247, Fat: 15 g, Carbs: 21g, Protein: 17g,

## *14). Lemon Salmon with White Beans*

4 5-ounce salmon filets

1/2 cup nonfat plain Greek yogurt

3/4 teaspoon paprika

2 teaspoons extra-virgin olive oil

4 cloves garlic, minced

1 tsp. dried Italian seasoning

1 lemon, halved

Red Pepper Flakes (optional)

3 cups cannellini beans (canned is easiest) (cooked, drained and rinsed)

Kosher salt and

Freshly ground black pepper

## Instructions:

1. Zest half of the lemon and set the zest aside. Squeeze the juice of that same half of the lemon into a small bowl (removing the seeds) and stir in the yogurt and paprika.
2. Heat the oil in a skillet, and sauté the garlic with the Italian seasoning and red pepper flakes if you're using them. Stir constantly so the garlic doesn't stick for about 3 minutes. Stir in the beans, salt, pepper, and lemon zest. And stir for another minute or two.
3. Season the salmon with salt and pepper and more paprika and bake on a foil covered baking pan under the broiler for about 7 minutes or until salmon reaches desired doneness.
4. Slice up the other half of the lemon into rounds and Serve the salmon filet over the beans and top with yogurt sauce and serve with lemon rounds.

**Prepping Instructions:** refrigerate in glass or Tupperware for up to 3 days. Heat in microwave or on the stove top before eating.

**Yield:** 4 servings

**Nutrition:** Calories: 393, Fat: 15.8 g, Carbohydrates: 14.7 g, Protein: 42.1 g.

## *15). Grilled Chicken with Homemade Tzatziki*

2 lbs boneless skinless chicken breast

¼ c. olive oil

2 tbsp. soy sauce

1/3 c. balsamic vinegar

1 tbsp. brown sugar

Black Pepper

Kosher Salt

*For the Tzatziki:*

1 cup Greek yogurt

½ cucumber, diced small

2 cloves garlic, minced very small

1 tablespoon lemon juice

1 teaspoon lemon zest plus

2 tablespoons chopped fresh dill

Kosher salt and freshly cracked black pepper

**Instructions:**
1. Season the chicken breasts with salt and pepper.
2. In a small bowl whisk together oil, soy sauce, balsamic vinegar, and brown sugar. Place the chicken breasts in a ziplock bag and pour in the sauce. Squish around the chicken so its all evenly coated and place the bag in the fridge for at least 30 minutes.
3. Meanwhile, prepare the Tzatziki sauce: combine the yogurt, garlic, lemon juice, lemon zest, dill, and salt and pepper to taste. Set aside.
4. When the grill is nice and hot, place the chicken on the grill and grill for 3-4 minutes on each side or until the meat thermometer reads 165 degrees. Allow the chicken to sit for 5-10 minutes before cutting and serving.

**Prepping Instructions:** you can marinate the chicken over night and cook the next day, or else store the grilled chicken in foil or glass in the fridge for up to 2 days. Heat in the microwave or eat cold with Tzatziki dipping sauce.

**Yield:** 4 servings

**Nutrition:** Calories: 314, Fat: 19.2 g, Carbohydrates: 7.9 g, Protein: 27.3 g.

## *16). Cauliflower Prawn Casserole*

¼ teaspoon crushed red pepper flakes

¼ teaspoon salt

2 cloves garlic

1 pound fresh raw shrimp, peeled and deveined

2 (14.5 ounce) cans fire roasted tomatoes

1 teaspoon lemon zest

½ cup feta cheese

1 tablespoon fresh dill, chopped

1 head of cauliflower

**Instructions:**

1. Break the cauliflower down into small florets and discard any big inedible stalks.
2. Mix cauliflower, onion, oil, pepper flakes and salt and spread the mixture in baking pan. Bake at 425 for 20-30 minutes.
3. Mix the shrimp with the lemon zest and the garlic, then pour over the cooked cauliflower mixture and put back in the oven and cook for 15 minutes more until the shrimp is pink and fully cooked.
4. Sprinkle the feta over the casserole and garnish with fresh dill.

**Prepping Instructions:** make the cauliflower crust and bake it, just add the shrimp fresh and cook right before eating — otherwise keep the shrimp separate from the cauliflower mixture.

**Yield:** 4 servings

**Nutrition:** Calories: 228, Fat: 6.6 g, Carbohydrates: 10.9 g, Protein: 30.9 g.

## *17). Halibut Beurre Blanc*

3 tablespoon extra-virgin olive oil

2 (8 ounce) halibut filets

1/2 cup white wine (chardonnay or equivalent)

2 teaspoon chopped garlic

2 Tablespoons of salted butter

½ tsp. kosher salt

¼ tsp. Cracked pepper

¼ cup capers

## Instructions:

1. Heat 2 tablespoons of olive oil in a skillet and pan fry the halibut searing on all sides until golden brown. Remove the fish from the pan and set on a plate.
2. Pour in the white wine and whisk making sure to scrape away any bits stuck on the bottom of the pan. Let the wine cook way down until all the alcohol has cooked off and you just have a small amount of liquid left and add the rest of the olive oil and all remaining ingredients and stir. Let it bubble up a bit then add the fish back to the pan and cook basting with the sauce until the fish is fully cooked and flakey.
3. Serve and pour the residual sauce over the fish and serve with lemon wedge and fresh dill sprig if desired. Serve with fresh vegetables of your choice

**Prepping Instructions:** you can make the wine sauce ahead and store in a glass jar, but you'll want to fry up the fish the day of. Keep the ingredients on hand and throw it together in a few minutes before eating.

**Yield:** 4 servings

**Nutrition:** Calories: 359, Fat: 30 g, Carbohydrates: 1 g, Protein: 15 g.

## *18). Polenta With Roasted Summer Vegetables*

2 tablespoons olive oil

1 bell pepper, seeded and chopped

1 eggplant, diced into small pieces

1 large zucchini, diced into small pieces

6 cups water

1 1/2 dry polenta

1 tablespoon butter, salted

1/4 teaspoon cracked black pepper

10 ounces frozen spinach, thawed and drained

½ cup cherry tomatoes, halved

¼ cup kalamata olives, chopped

1 tsp. dried Italian seasoning

## Instructions:

1. Toss the eggplant zucchini and peppers in one tbsp. of olive oil and spread over a cookie sheet. Place under the broiler on low in the center rack. When the vegetables start to caramelize and become tender remove from the oven.
2. In a medium pot, boil the water and stir in the dry polenta. Cook and stir as it thickens for about 5 minutes. Once the mixture gets thick and custardy, stir in the butter and black pepper.
3. Spread the polenta batter into a greased square baking pan and brush the top with olive oil. Bake at 350 for about 10 minutes.
4. Top with spinach and then add the tomatoes and olives, and next the roasted vegetables and finally the Italian seasoning. Add kosher salt to taste. Bake for 10 more minutes, and then slice into wedges and serve.

**Prepping Instructions:** You can make the roasted vegetables and the polenta crust ahead of time and store in the fridge for up to 3 days. Assemble the day of and bake at 350 for 10 minutes and serve.

**Yield:** 4 servings

**Nutrition:** Calories: 223, Fat: 11.9 g, Carbohydrates: 27.8 g, Protein: 5.9 g.

## 19). *Spanakopita Egg Bake*

1/4 c. olive oil

1 large onion, chopped finely

2 cups baby spinach, chopped

2 cups swiss chard, chopped very small

Kosher Salt

Freshly ground black pepper

½ c. feta cheese

4 eggs

**Instructions:**

1. Preheat oven to 350 and grease a baking pan
2. Sauté the onion in the olive oil over medium heat in a skillet until tender and translucent. Add in the spinach swiss chard. Add in salt and pepper. Pour the mixture into the baking dish
3. Sprinkle the feta over the greens. In another bowl, lightly beat the eggs and then pour the eggs over the spinach feta mixture.
4. Bake for 20 minutes until set and top is golden brown. Serve warm

**Prepping Instructions:** store in glass or metal pan covered with foil for up to 3 days. Heat in the oven before eating.

**Yield:** 4 servings

**Nutrition:** Calories: 242, Fat: 21.8 g, Carbohydrates: 5.1 g, Protein: 9.4 g.

## 20). Vegetable Thin Crust Pizza

*Crust:*

1 1/4 cup whole wheat flour

1/2 teaspoon yeast

1/2 cup hot water

2 tsp. honey

Pinch of salt

*Toppings:*

1/2 cup Greek yogurt

1/2 cup tomato sauce

1 olive oil

½ tsp. garlic powder

1/4 teaspoon oregano

1 1/2 cup shredded mozzarella

1/4 cup black olives, chopped

½ c. green onions

1 cup sliced cremini mushrooms

1 cup spinach, chopped

1 small tomato sliced in rounds

**Instructions:**

1. Mix yeast and honey and add the warm water—make sure the water isn't too hot. Should be cool enough to hold your finger in. Allow the yeast to activate and foam up then pour

into a bowl. Add in the flower and a drizzle of olive oil. Mix and roll the dough into a ball.

2. Allow the dough to rise for 10-15 minutes, then punch it down
3. Spread the crust very thinly over a baking sheet or pizza stone and bake for 5 minutes at 425 degrees.
4. Meanwhile, mix together the yogurt and tomato sauce garlic powder, oregano, salt and pepper.
5. Spread this sauce over the crust, then add the cheese and toppings.
6. Bake 10-15 minutes until the crust is crispy and the cheese is melted.

**Prepping Instructions:** Make the pizza crust ahead and bake the first 5 minutes as indicated in step 3. Then you can store the crust for up to 4 days, or freeze for later use. Then the day of, all you have to do is pour on the sauce and toppings and bake for 10-15 minutes and then serve.

**Yield:** 4 servings

**Nutrition:** Calories: 266, Fat: 7.6 g, Carbohydrates: 39.6 g, Protein: 11.4 g.

## *21). One-Pan Honey Lemon Chicken*

1 lb. boneless skinless chicken breasts

1/2 teaspoon salt, pepper to taste

2 olive oil

1/4 cup flour

½ tsp. black pepper

1-2 cups chopped asparagus

2 lemons, sliced

1 tsp. lemon zest

2 tablespoons butter

2 tablespoons honey

**Instructions:**

1. Mix the flour with salt and pepper and then dredge the chicken in the flour.
2. Heat the oil in a large skillet and pan fry the chicken 3-5 minutes on each side seasoning with the fresh cracked pepper.
3. Remove the chicken from the pan and add the asparagus and saute until the color brightens and the asparagus becomes slightly tender, then transfer to a plate.
4. Next lightly brown the lemon slices in the pan and remove them to the plate.
5. Mix the lemon zest honey and 2 tablespoons of butter and melt the butter whisking the sauce until it's bubbly and combined.
6. Serve the chicken with the asparagus and top with lemon slices and drizzle the butter sauce on top.

**Prepping Instructions:** store in a glass container for up to 3 days in the fridge. Heat in the oven or microwave before eating.

**Yield:** 4 servings

**Nutrition:** Calories: 402, Fat: 21.3 g, Carbohydrates: 18.8 g, Protein: 34.8 g.

## 22). *Harvest Pumpkin Lentil Soup*

1 tsbsp. Olive Oil

2 onions, diced

3 cloves garlic, minced

2 tbsp. tomato paste

¼ c. fresh cilantro, chopped

1/2 tsp ground cumin

¼ tsp. ground ginger

½ tsp. fresh ground black pepper (or to taste)

1 tsp. kosher salt (or to taste)

1 cup lentils, dry

15 oz can pumpkin puree

4 c. vegetable stock

Salt

1/2 fresh lemon, juice of

1/4 cup pine nuts, toasted in olive oil

1/4 C. Greek Yogurt

**Instrctions:**

1. Saute the onions in 1 tbps. Of olive oil over medium heat in the bottom of a large pot for 4 minutes or until the onions start to turn translucent. Add the garlic and stir for another minute until garlic is fragrant. Stir in tomato paste, cilantro, salt, pepper and cumin
2. Stir in the pumpkin puree, vegetable stock, and lentils. Bring to a boil and allow it to boil gently, stirring, for 5 minutes.
3. Reduce heat and simmer with the lid propped for 15-20 minutes or until the lentils are fully cooked and tender.
4. Pour the mixture into a blender and pulse until well incorporated and until lentils are broken down.
5. Return to the pot and add the lemon juice, reheating and cooking for 5 more minutes.
6. Serve with a dollop of greek yogurt on top and sprinkled toasted pine nuts.

**Prepping Instructions:** Simply reheat on the stove top when you're ready to eat. Top with the yogurt and pine nuts only just before eating. Store in glass for up to 3-4 days in the fridge.

**Yield:** 4 servings

**Nutrition:** Calories: 330, Fat: 10 g, Carbohydrates: 44 g, Protein: 17 g.

## 23). Zoodle Greek Pasta Salad

2 zucchini, spiralized or cut into noodles

½ small cucumber, diced

1 c. grape tomatoes, halved

½ c. red onion, sliced thin

½ c. crumbled feta

½ c. sliced black olives

*Yogurt Dressing:*

1/4 cup Greek yogurt

2 cloves garlic, minced

1 teaspoon lemon zest

2 tablespoon lemon juice

2 tablespoon olive oil

¼ tsp red pepper flakes (or to taste)

1 teaspoon honey

Salt and fresh ground black pepper

**Instructions:**

1. Spiralize the zucchini if you have a vegetable spiraler. If you don't have one buy one! They're awesome. But otherwise, you can use a potato peeler and peel the zucchini into medium thickness ribbons or use a sharp knife and chop it into noodles, but the spiraler is definitely the best option.

2. Toss together zucchini noodles, cucumber, tomato, onion, feta and olives.
3. In a separate bowl, whisk together all the dressing ingredients.
4. When ready to serve, pour the dressing over the zucchini noodle mixture and toss until the vegetables are well coated.

**Prepping Instructions:** keep the salad and the dressing separate and mix together only when you're ready to serve. Store in glass in the fridge for up to 3 days.

**Yield:** 4 servings

**Nutrition:** Calories: 184, Fat: 13.4 g, Carbohydrates: 12.1 g, Protein: 6.2 g.

## *24). Oven Baked Stuffed Zucchini*

1 large zucchini

2 tablespoons olive oil

½ onion, diced

3 cloves garlic, minced

1/2 lb lean ground turkey

1 14.5 oz can fire roasted tomatoes

1 cup quinoa, cooked

1/2 teaspoon ground cumin

1 tsp. dried Italian Seasoning

Salt & pepper to taste

1 tablespoon tahini

1 teaspoon lemon juice

**Instructions:**
1. Slice in half lengthwise and remove the stem. Scoop out some of the center with the seeds to make room for the filling.
2. Brush with 1 tablespoon of the olive oil and season lightly with salt and pepper. Bake on a greased cookie sheet at 425 degrees for 20-25 minutes.
3. Meanwhile, sauté the onion and garlic in the other tablespoon of olive oil in a skillet over medium heat until onions begin to soften (about 3-4 minutes). Make sure the garlic doesn't stick to the bottom or it will scorch. Add the ground turkey and stir breaking it up until fully cooked and crumbly.
4. Add the can of tomatoes (including juice), quinoa, cumin, Italian Seasoning, salt and pepper and mix. Simmer until heated through and the mixture starts to bubble.
5. Remove the cooked zucchini from the oven and stuff with the turkey quinoa mixture. Bake for 10 more minutes at 350 degrees.
6. Mix the tahini and lemon juice and drizzle over the baked stuffed zucchini before servings.

**Prepping Instructions:** To prepare ahead, proceed all the way to step 5, but don't bake for the final 10 minutes. Wrap stuffed zucchini in foil and store in the fridge for up to 3 days. When ready to serve, heat in the oven at 350 for 15-20 minutes and top with the tahini mixture.

**Yield:** 4 servings

**Nutrition:** Calories: 377, Fat: 17 g, Carbohydrates: 38 g, Protein: 20 g.

## *25). Eggplant Pesto Casserole*

1 large eggplant cut into cubes

1 onion, diced

1 (6oz) package baby bella mushrooms, washed and halved

1 cup cherry tomatoes red and yellow, halved

1 lg bell pepper, chopped

8 oz whole wheat penne (or pasta of your choice)

¼ c prepared pesto

¼ c fresh parmesan, hand grated

½ c. shredded mozzarella

¼ c. fresh basil, roughly chopped

## Instructions:

1. Coat eggplant, onions, peppers, mushrooms and tomatoes in olive oil and season with salt and pepper.
2. Roast on a baking sheet under the broiler for 15-20 minutes or until the vegetables start to caramelize. Stir up the pan once or twice during the cooking process to make sure the vegetables roast on all sides.
3. Meanwhile, cook the pasta per package instructions (boil with a pinch of salt). Drain.
4. In a bowl toss the pasta with the roasted vegetables, pesto and basil.

5. Pour into a greased square baking dish and top with the cheese. Bake about 20 minutes covered at 350 degrees (or until cheese is melted and the dish is hot and slightly bubbly.

**Prepping Instructions:** you can prepare the casserole ahead of time and assemble and simply refrigerate covered with foil for up to 3 days. Bake right before eating. Alternatively, you can freeze the casserole and thaw and bake later.

**Yield:** 4 servings
**Nutrition:** Calories: 430, Fat: 14 g, Carbohydrates: 45 g, Protein: 22 g.

# Conclusion:

Thank you for joining me on this journey. I hope you've enjoyed reading this book and especially I hope you've enjoyed the recipes. Many of them are my adaption of old family recipes that have long been cherished by me and my people.

With the breakneck speed the world is moving at these days, it is so important to take the time out of our busy lives to take care of ourselves. In a nutshell, that's the essence of the Mediterranean lifestyle. I'm so grateful you've made the admirable and wise decision to protect and foster the most valuable resource you have: your health.

If you like this book, I humbly ask for your honest feedback by leaving me a review about my book. Even more importantly, spread the word. Share what you've learned with your loved ones. I'm sure we all know many who could benefit from the Mediterranean lifestyle.

Wishing you and your loved ones all the best in health!

Saluti!

-Maureen Sarkis

Made in the USA
San Bernardino, CA
25 June 2018